HAL•LEONARD
INSTRUMENTAL
PLAY-ALONG

TRUMPET

AUDIO
ACCESS
INCLUDED

PLAYBACK+
Speed • Pitch • Balance • Loop

FAVORITE Disney SONGS

T0085247

Audio arrangements by Peter Deneff

To access audio, visit:
www.halleonard.com/mylibrary

Enter Code
6210-5305-1911-3971

ISBN 978-1-70514-272-1

HAL•LEONARD®

Visit Hal Leonard Online at
www.halleonard.com

Contact us:
Hal Leonard
7777 West Bluemound Road
Milwaukee, WI 53213
Email: info@halleonard.com

In Europe, contact:
Hal Leonard Europe Limited
42 Wigmore Street
Marylebone, London, W1U 2RN
Email: info@halleonardeurope.com

In Australia, contact:
Hal Leonard Australia Pty. Ltd.
4 Lentara Court
Cheltenham, Victoria, 3192 Australia
Email: info@halleonard.com.au

CONTENTS

THE BALLAD OF THE LONESOME COWBOY

from TOY STORY 4

TRUMPET

Music and Lyrics by
RANDY NEWMAN

EVERMORE
from BEAUTY AND THE BEAST

Music by ALAN MENKEN
Lyrics by TIM RICE

TRUMPET

Sturdy Ballad

HOW DOES A MOMENT LAST FOREVER

from BEAUTY AND THE BEAST

TRUMPET

Music by ALAN MENKEN
Lyrics by TIM RICE

HOW FAR I'LL GO
from MOANA

TRUMPET

Music and Lyrics by
LIN-MANUEL MIRANDA

INTO THE UNKNOWN

from FROZEN 2

TRUMPET

Music and Lyrics by KRISTEN ANDERSON-LOPEZ
and ROBERT LOPEZ

IT'S ALL RIGHT

featured in SOUL

Words and Music by
CURTIS MAYFIELD

TRUMPET

LAVA
from LAVA

TRUMPET

Music and Lyrics by
JAMES FORD MURPHY

LEAD THE WAY
from RAYA AND THE LAST DRAGON

TRUMPET

Music and Lyrics by
JHENÉ AIKO

THE PLACE WHERE LOST THINGS GO

from MARY POPPINS RETURNS

TRUMPET

Music by MARC SHAIMAN
Lyrics by SCOTT WITTMAN and MARC SHAIMAN

NEVER TOO LATE
from THE LION KING 2019

Music by ELTON JOHN
Lyrics by TIM RICE

TRUMPET

SPEECHLESS
from ALADDIN (2019)

Music by ALAN MENKEN
Lyrics by BENJ PASEK
and JUSTIN PAUL

TRUMPET

Moderately

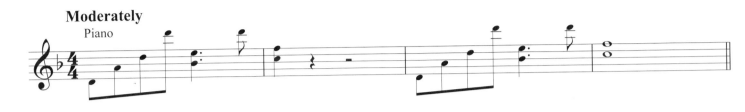

TOUCH THE SKY
from BRAVE

TRUMPET

Music by ALEXANDER L. MANDEL
Lyrics by ALEXANDER L. MANDEL
and MARK ANDREWS

With spirit

Fiddle and pipe

TRY EVERYTHING
from ZOOTOPIA

Words and Music by SIA FURLER,
TOR ERIK HERMANSEN and MIKKEL ERIKSEN

TRUMPET

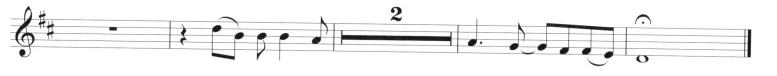

YOU'RE WELCOME
from MOANA

TRUMPET

Music and Lyrics by
LIN-MANUEL MIRANDA

REMEMBER ME
(Ernesto de la Cruz)
from COCO

TRUMPET

Words and Music by KRISTEN ANDERSON-LOPEZ
and ROBERT LOPEZ